Do You Know?

HOW
HISTORY BEGAN

By
Philip Sauvain
Illustrated by
Jim Robins

Warwick Press
New York/London/Toronto/Sydney
1985

Contents

If we keep a diary we are writing down a history of our own lives. In recent times much of what has happened in the world has been written down in books and newspapers. So it is quite easy for us to find out about these events.

But people have been living on the earth for many thousands of years — long before there were books or newspapers — and it is these ancient people that we will be looking at here.

People who study ancient history today must search for clues from objects that have been left behind. They look for the bones of ancient people, and for the tools, pottery and metal objects they made. From these remains historians can piece together a picture of how our history began.

ISBN: 0-531-19005-6

Library of Congress Catalog Card No. 85-50759

Published in 1985 by Warwick Press, 387 Park Avenue South, New York, New York 10016.
First published in 1985 by Piper Books Ltd., London.
Copyright © by Piper Books Ltd., 1985
All rights reserved
Printed in Spain.
5 4 3 2 1

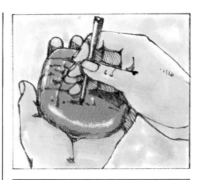
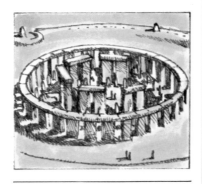

1 The First Humans

No one knows for certain who the first humans were. This is because very few remains have been found. One small group of human beings lived in Africa about 1½ million years ago. They looked more like apes than people and ate berries and fruit and any small animals they could catch. Yet they were more skillful than animals because they had discovered that they could use stones and sticks as simple weapons.

The next big step was to learn how to make tools. By about 500,000 years ago, people in China were using simple chopping tools made from hard stones, like flint. They had also discovered how to use fire — both for warmth and, possibly, for cooking meat.

As time passed these early humans slowly improved their stone tools and wooden spears. They discovered that if they hunted in groups they could use their weapons to kill bigger animals and then everyone could share the meat. They also found out how to skin the dead animals and use the skins for clothes. Clothes had become important. The weather in many parts of the world was gradually getting colder and colder — it was the beginning of an Ice Age.

Because the first humans made their tools out of stone we call them the Stone Age people. The Stone Age lasted for a very long time. But the basic way of making the tools remained the same. At first, one stone was simply knocked against another one to give it a sharp broken edge. Later on, stone hand-axes were made by using pieces of bone or hard wood to chip away flakes of flint. This gave a sharp edge and a point.

2 The Cave Dwellers

About 70,000 years ago, groups of human beings lived in caves along the edges of the ice fields which stretched all the way across Europe. They are known as the Neanderthal people.

Whole family groups shared one large cave. A fire at the entrance to the cave helped to keep the people inside warm. It also helped to frighten wild animals away.

The tools used by the Neanderthal people were more advanced than those of the earlier Stone Age people. They knew how to sharpen a wooden spear to a hard point. They shaped the end with a flint axe and then heated the end in a fire.

They used sharp flint tools to cut up meat and to scrape the flesh away from animal skins. Skins were then hung up to dry, probably by stretching them across wooden frames.

The Neanderthal people would have hunted reindeer and wild cattle. If they were lucky, they might manage to kill a woolly rhinoceros. A successful hunt could keep a family alive for many weeks.

Later in the Stone Age, people may have begun to believe in magic. Hunting was a matter of life or death, and some people drew pictures of the animals they hunted on the walls of caves. These cave painters may have hoped their drawings would help the hunters to kill a lot of animals.

It is possible that the Neanderthal people were the first to wonder what happened to someone when he or she died. They may even have had a religion. The remains of burials show that they buried their dead carefully. They placed the body in a grave so that it rested on its side. It was then covered with reddish powder.

First of all the cave painters drew an outline of the animal on the cave walls. They used a sharp flint or a piece of charcoal — soft burned wood.

Then they ground up lumps of soft colored rocks or earths into powders. They mixed the powders with water or animal fat to make paints.

They probably used twigs or bunches of grass to spread the paint over their drawings. But sometimes they just used their fingers.

3 The Hunters

After a great many years, the Ice Age finally ended. During that time the Neanderthal people had all disappeared, and different types of people had taken their place.

By about 10,000 years ago, groups of these people were living in wooden shelters alongside rivers and lakes in northern Europe. They lived mainly by hunting and they used bows and arrows as well as spears.

Both the arrows and the spears were tipped with sharp pieces of flint. An arrow could be fired further and faster than a spear could be thrown. This meant the hunters could wound an animal before the rest of the herd knew they were near. Then they would use their spears to finish it off.

The hunters had discovered how to make boats, by scooping out the middle of a tree trunk. To catch fish they used a spear with a jagged point that hooked into the fish. They also made nets which they used at the water's edge.

Other members of the group would have collected the fruits, nuts and berries that grew wild in the forests and marshes around their shelters. Everyone had to work hard to make sure that there was enough to eat every day.

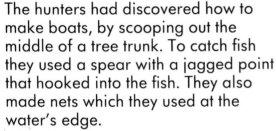

These Stone Age people still used flint tools for scraping and cutting, but they made use of many other things too. They wove simple baskets and mats from the reeds and rushes that grew near the water. They had learned how to make needles from splinters of bone. With needles and thin strips of leather they could sew skins together to make better clothes. They had even hit on the idea of using trained dogs to help them hunt the deer, elk and wild pigs of the forests.

4 The First Farmers

Wheat was originally a wild plant of the Middle East. People would cut and gather it with a sharp, curved stone tool called a sickle. Then they ground the grains to make wheat flour.

The grinding was done by hand, crushing the grains between two round slabs of stone called a quern. Sometimes, grains fell to the ground nearby and grew into new plants.

Farming began when people started to plant these wheat grains on purpose. They hoed the ground first to break up the soil and make it soft. This made it easier to sow the seeds.

As well as crops, people began to farm animals. Instead of hunting them in the wild as before, they built fences to keep them near at hand. Sheep and goats were some of the first animals to be kept in this way.

Milk made butter and cheese. Wool was spun and woven into cloth. And, of course, animals were killed for food. Farmers also discovered that animals could be used to carry or pull heavy loads.

The idea of farming food rather than hunting or gathering it spread quickly around the hot countries of the Middle East.

The farmers soon learned that their crops needed plenty of sun to ripen. They also discovered that they needed regular watering too. Because of this many farmers lived alongside the main rivers in these lands, like the Nile and the Tigris. Here, instead of carrying the water to the fields they dug ditches in the earth to let it flow straight from the river. This way of watering crops is called irrigation.

Stone Age hunters had to travel from place to place in search of food, following the herds of wild animals as they moved across the land. A few farmers also traveled in this way,

moving their herds of cows to new grazing areas. But most Stone Age farmers stayed in one place, close to their crops and their animals. For the first time, it was worth building proper houses to live in.

The walls of the houses were built with wet mud and clay from the river banks. The mud was then left to dry out in the sun until it baked hard, like brick. The roofs were thatched with wood and straw and there were narrow slits in the walls for windows. The houses were cool and shady in the summer heat.

11

5 The First Towns

Sometimes, farmers found that they had more food than they needed. Other people discovered that they were better at making things, like tools and cloth, than they were at farming. Before long, farmers were exchanging their extra food for these goods.

In some places craftsmen and farmers lived near to each other, in small villages. If a village was near a river or a place that was easy to get to, it might grow into a town.

Some people found that if they traveled about buying goods from other places and bringing them to a town, people would come from all around to trade with them. These were the first merchants.

In time, a few towns became so wealthy the people needed soldiers to defend them. The leader of the soldiers often took control of the town and the farms around it and became their king or ruler.

A few towns grew so large and powerful they became cities. One of these was the City of Ur in Sumer, on the banks of the Euphrates river.

One king of Ur, called Ur-Nammu, built a huge brick tower in the city about 4,100 years ago. The tower had a temple to the gods on top and was shaped like a stepped pyramid. We call it a ziggurat.

Imagine a busy market day in Ur. Craftsmen and merchants of all kinds shout their wares. A group of soldiers parade through the streets, while visiting farmers and curious townsfolk look on.

Pottery was one of the greatest inventions of all time. The first potter may have got the idea after seeing how moist clay becomes hard when it is heated.

The first pots may have been just lumps of clay, hollowed out into a bowl shape. Then people found that it was easier to shape the pots if they built them up out of coils of clay — like coiling rope. The edges of the coils were then smoothed over to make a flat surface which could be decorated by scratching patterns into the clay, or painting it.

The wet pots were hardened in the sun or in the ashes of a fire.

It was the people of Sumer who invented the potter's wheel. This made it easier to turn a clay ball into a smooth even-shaped pot. The Sumerian potters baked their pots in a kiln. This was a hot oven lined with bricks to keep the heat in.

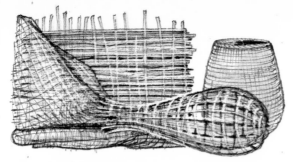

Stone Age hunters had woven baskets and nets from reeds and tough grasses. When people started to keep sheep and goats they discovered they could weave the hair from these animals too.

Long strands of the hair or wool first had to be combed straight and then twisted together to make the yarn or thread. This is called spinning.

Cloth was woven from the yarn by hanging lengths of it on a wooden frame called a loom. Weights tied to the bottom of each length kept it tight. Other lengths of yarn were then threaded from side to side, between the hanging lengths.

About 5,000 years ago the Sumerians also invented writing by making wedge-shaped marks in small tablets of clay. They used it to keep records of all the goods the people paid to their king. At first, the marks looked like small pictures of the objects they stood for. But slowly the marks became just patterns, symbols, which stood for the objects.

	BIRD			
	FISH			
	OX			
	WHEAT			

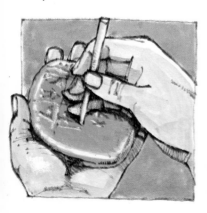

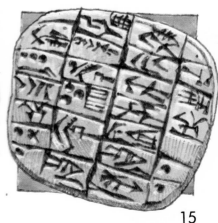

⑦ Using Metals

Learning to use metals made an enormous difference to the lives of our early ancestors.

Metals are usually found in a mixture of rock and earth called ore. The very first metalworkers probably picked up lumps of ore by accident and found that when heated to a high temperature, the metal in the ore became liquid. Then, when the metal had cooled and hardened it could be beaten into different shapes, which, unlike clay, could not be easily cracked or broken. Also, there were different kinds of metal, like copper and tin.

People began to mine the ore. They dug it out of the ground with picks

made from antlers. Lumps of ore were taken in baskets to a furnace. Leather bellows were pumped by foot to send air into the furnace to make the fire glow white with heat.

When the metal in the ore melted it was collected and poured carefully into clay molds where it was allowed to cool. Molds could be made to give the metal whatever shape was needed. They could make weapons such as swords and daggers, or tools like ax-heads or knife blades. Metal tools and weapons could be given a sharp point or a sharp edge and they lasted longer than those made of flint. In battle, the

metal weapons were much more powerful.

Sometimes metal was cast into a lump called an ingot. This was later heated slightly until soft and then hammered into the right shape. Softer metals like gold and silver were often used like this to make beautiful ornaments and jewelry.

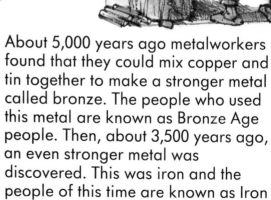

About 5,000 years ago metalworkers found that they could mix copper and tin together to make a stronger metal called bronze. The people who used this metal are known as Bronze Age people. Then, about 3,500 years ago, an even stronger metal was discovered. This was iron and the people of this time are known as Iron Age people.

8 The Spread of Civilization

Northern Europe

The new skills of farming, pottery, weaving, writing and the use of metals spread very slowly across the world. In places like northern Europe, for example, where the weather was cold and harsh, people had to work very hard just to get enough to eat. They had little time to learn new skills. While magnificent cities were springing up in other parts of the

Northern Europe

Rome

Athens

Mediterranean

Egypt   Baby

Rome

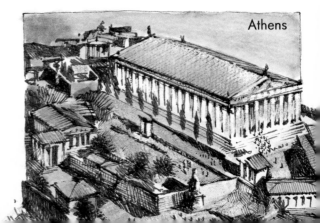

Egypt

Athens

world, the northern people were still living in small villages of roughly built thatched huts.

At different times, these cities, such as Athens and Rome, became the centers of great civilizations that ruled the ancient world.

Babylon   Indus Valley   China

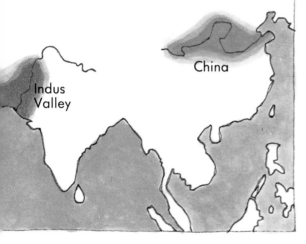

The first civilizations, like Egypt and Babylon, all grew up around fertile river valleys in the Middle East and in parts of Asia and, later, around the Mediterranean Sea. All of these places had warm climates where it was easy to grow crops. Here, farmers produced large harvests, with plenty to spare to feed people who lived in towns and cities.

Some of these civilizations lasted for thousands of years, others for a few hundred.

The city of Babylon began to be built over 4,000 years ago, along the banks of the Euphrates river. A king called Hammurabi made Babylon the capital of an empire which ruled all the land along the valley. It was at the height of its power about 2,600 years ago, under a king called Nebuchadnezzar.

In Asia, two other great cities, Harappa and Mohenjo-daro were also being built about 4,000 years ago. They lay along the banks of the Indus river, in an area that is now part of Pakistan. The Indus valley people were very good builders. Their cities were carefully planned and laid out in straight lines. Rich people's houses were built of brick and even had drains and bathrooms.

About 3,500 years ago, a civilization was founded in China by people known as the Shang. The Shang lived beside the Hwang-ho river and were ruled by warrior kings. About this time too, American Indians began to farm the land.

Gods And Kings: Egypt

The greatest of all the ancient civilizations arose in Egypt about 5,000 years ago.

The Egyptians owed everything to the Nile river. Every year in spring it flooded, bringing water to the fields and leaving behind a layer of rich silt which made the fields very fertile.

For the rest of the year the farmers took water from the river with the help of a shaduf. This was a bucket on a swinging pole. A weight at the other end made it easy to lift the heavy bucket, swing it around and pour the water into an irrigation ditch.

The river flood made it possible for Egyptian farmers to grow enough food to feed the thousands of soldiers,

priests, servants and officials who served the Egyptian king. The king and his rich nobles lived in splendid houses. Inside them they had baths and lavatories and many luxuries we think of as being modern inventions.

The Pharaohs (the name we usually give the kings of Egypt) were worshiped as gods by their people.

When a Pharaoh died his body was taken by the priests and soaked in a special liquid to preserve it. Then the body was wrapped tightly around with many layers of bandages. Sometimes, a death mask of precious metal was put over the face. We call a body that has been treated like this a "mummy." Some Egyptian mummies still exist in museums today.

The Egyptians also built enormous stone tombs for the Pharaohs called pyramids. Each pyramid would have taken many years to complete.

When the mummy of the dead Pharaoh was ready it was taken by boat down the Nile to the pyramid. A great procession of priests carried it from the boat to the burial chamber, which was usually hidden deep in the heart of the pyramid.

The Egyptians believed in life after death. So gold ornaments, tools, furniture, pottery, food and a great many other useful things were placed in the burial chamber too. They were all for the dead Pharaoh to use in the next world.

10 The Northern Tribes

Around 4,000 years ago there were no pyramids or great kings in northern Europe. Nor were there cities like Mohenjo-daro and Babylon.

The people who lived in this part of the world found it much harder to grow crops. Summers were short and there was less sun to ripen the harvests. Also, much of the land was covered by huge forests. At first, many farmers just kept herds of sheep and cattle instead of growing wheat as a main source of food.

Although the knowledge of metalworking took some time to reach them, the northern tribes soon became skilled at making copper and bronze weapons and tools. Bronze Age farmers and craftsmen lived in villages of small round huts made from earth, stone or wood. There would have been an opening in one side for a door, but no windows. As well as eating and sleeping in their huts, people cooked inside them too. It must have been very dark and smoky inside, and very damp in winter.

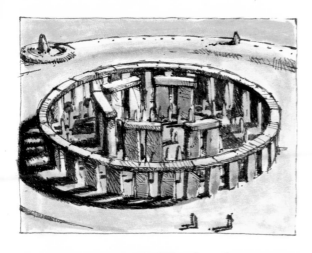

In spite of their houses, however, the northern tribes were, in fact, very skilled at building large stone monuments. It is probable that these monuments were organized by priests. Complicated circles and lines of huge upright stones have been found all over northern and western Europe. Some of them, such as Stonehenge in Britain, were built over hundreds of years, but no one is sure what they were for.

The huge stones that make up Stonehenge were dragged to the site on wooden sleds and rollers by hundreds of people. They were then lowered into deep pits.

The pits were filled in to keep the stones upright. Another stone was placed alongside two uprights and a platform of logs slowly built up under it.

When the platform was high enough the third stone was carefully levered on top of the other two. Stonehenge was finally finished about 3,500 years ago.

It was not until about 2,800 years ago that iron came into use in northern Europe. By this time, northern metalworkers had become highly skilled at making ornaments and jewelry as well as weapons and tools. Iron weapons were far stronger and sharper than bronze. They were used by a group of people known as the Celts who began to spread through Europe. They were ferocious warriors who fought with shields, helmets, swords and spears.

11 Writers And Thinkers: Greece

By about 2,500 years ago, a great civilization had grown up in Greece. The Greeks lived in cities, like Athens, Sparta and Thebes. Each city had its own government in which every man who was a citizen (that is, a free man of the city and not a slave) had a vote. The citizens met in special buildings to talk about which laws were to be made and how they were to be governed. The most powerful city was Athens, which had many fine buildings and temples.

The Greeks lived in a country that was hilly and hard to farm. Instead, their wealth came from the sea. They were skilled sailors and merchants. They traded with other countries everywhere along the coast of the Mediterranean Sea and the Black Sea, taking their ideas with them as well as their goods.

The Greeks were famous for their scientific discoveries. They were the first to work out that the world was round. Yet they had no way of traveling around the earth to prove if they were right.

A thinker called Euclid discovered how to use geometry. Others, like Socrates and Plato taught people to examine the way the world worked.

The Greeks placed a lot of importance on education. Boys were sent to school. Girls were taught at home by their mothers.

The Greeks were great lovers of sports and sporting contests. They thought everyone should be physically fit. Athletes always competed naked, except for some races where they carried shields and helmets to make the race more difficult. The most famous contest of all was held every four years at a place called Olympia. These were the first Olympic Games.

As well as trading ships, the Greeks had warships known as galleys. They were rowed through the water using long banks of oars on either side of the ship. The biggest, called triremes, had three banks on each side.

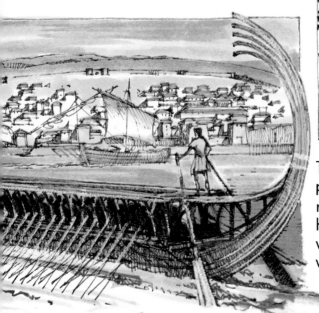

The Greeks also enjoyed watching plays and they built huge theaters with rows of stone seats cut into the sides of hills. All the actors were men, who wore masks to show which part they were playing.

12 The Empire Builders: Rome

The lands around the Mediterranean also saw the rise of the greatest empire of the ancient world. In time, the empire of Rome swallowed up the Greek civilization, and a great many others as well.

Rome began as a small village about 2,700 years ago. It perched on top of one of seven hills in the valley of the Tiber river in Italy. But Rome grew swiftly in importance.

By about 2,000 years ago, Rome had become a huge city. Half a million people may have lived there. The rich lived in large and luxurious houses on the hills, while the poor lived in crowded slums.

In the center of Rome there were many fine temples, shops, public bath-houses, theaters and squares.

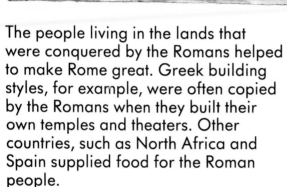

The people living in the lands that were conquered by the Romans helped to make Rome great. Greek building styles, for example, were often copied by the Romans when they built their own temples and theaters. Other countries, such as North Africa and Spain supplied food for the Roman people.

If you could have visited Rome 2,000 years ago you would probably have seen people from many different lands in its streets, such as Jews from Palestine, Egyptians, Africans and Celts from the northern lands.

The great wealth and power of Rome was due almost entirely to its army. The Roman army was the largest and most well-trained that the world had yet seen. Roman soldiers were trained to be fearless in battle. They were organized in legions of about 6,000 men. The legions were split into groups of 100 soldiers called a century. Each century had its own leader known as a centurion.

With this army Rome conquered and held an enormous empire.

27

13 Life In Roman Times

Wherever they lived the Romans took their own style of housing and way of life. In towns, the houses were usually two storeys high and built around a central courtyard. Often, a shop would form part of the ground floor of the house.

The Roman legions built forts in the lands which they conquered. Forts were usually rectangular in shape with stone walls and four main gateways, one on each side. The shape was so even that from above they would have looked like giant playing cards.

Within the strong stone walls were barracks where the ordinary soldiers lived. There was also a villa, or house, for the commanding officer. There were granaries in which enough wheat was stored to feed the soldiers during a long siege, and there would have been a well inside the walls too. Hospitals, workshops and other buildings made up the rest of the camp.

Very often, local people lived in huts near the fort for protection. Outside its walls they set up shops to serve the soldiers. Eventually some forts grew into busy towns, but the towns still had stone walls and strong gateways.

Wealthy people lived in country houses or fine town houses. They had costly mosaic-patterned floors in their main rooms. The rooms would also have been heated by warm air carried under the floors. Large banquets were given at which the guests ate lying on long couches.

In the kitchens, many of the pots and pans were similar to those we use today.

There were knives, ladles, colanders to strain vegetables, stewing pots and saucepans. The oven was often made of brick, with a hole underneath for a charcoal fire.

Every Roman town had public baths for its citizens. People visited the baths every day and met friends there. First they sat in hot steam rooms and hot baths. Slaves rubbed oils into their skins and scraped off the dirt. Then they cooled off in cold rooms and had cold baths.

At the height of its power the Roman Empire stretched from Britain in the north to Africa in the south. It included all the lands around the Mediterranean from Spain to the Middle East.

14 Digging Up History

We know about the distant past from what we find buried in the earth. People who dig up ancient remains are called archaeologists.

Imagine a village of baked mud huts about 6,000 years ago. Rubbish collects as people throw their broken pots and other things away. In time, even the houses fall down. They are replaced by new houses, built on top of the old.

Years later the village may be abandoned. Everything is slowly covered over by growing plants. In time, the dust and soil build up and the village is completely buried.

Some time later, another village, or even a town, grows up in the same place. This village may be destroyed by raiders. Then it too crumbles and becomes buried.

Each time a village rises and falls in this way another layer of remains is left hidden under the ground. Then one day they are found and give us vital clues about the past.

Archaeologists start their work by carefully digging a shallow trench. Slowly they remove each layer of earth to uncover the remains beneath. Walls are left as they are, but cleaned up to make it easy to see what the rooms would have looked like.

Bits of broken pottery are glued together to discover what sort of bowls the people used. Finds of tools and weapons are carefully cleaned. Bit by bit the archaeologists piece together the past.

Written records are even better at telling us about the past. Through them we have learned how the ancient Egyptians and Sumerians lived. The Egyptians wrote on papyrus (a type of paper). They used a special picture language called hieroglyphics. It was rather like the wedge-shaped writing used by Sumerians.

The great civilizations also left behind pictures and carvings which show us different events from people's everyday lives.

One of the most famous finds ever made was the Egyptian treasures of Tutankhamen.

Tutankhamen was a boy prince. When he died he was put in a burial chamber together with many gold ornaments and other priceless objects.

Index